Threebagsfulled presents

A Midsummer Knit's Dream

9 fabulous shawl patterns to get you from the heat of the beach to an evening garden party

from the creator of CRIMINAL KNITS

© 2013 Hilary Designs

Acknowledgments:

I blame this book on all the "Serial Knitters" who insisted I write it. You know who you are, so there's no wriggling out of it, and no complaining about how long it took. It's not my fault it rained every single time we scheduled a photo shoot!

I also suppose this means that Basketcase is officially off the hook for this one, although she still managed to keep me sane and focused throughout all the shenanigans, despite everything that was going on in her own world.

For her council to "take things easy" this year (which, of course, I quite obviously ignored) while she kept things running smoothly on CK for me, mega hugs to Kath Baer who knows what it's like to send the oldest one off to college for the first time. Again, CK would not exist without her. She really is the "Quietheart" in my never-ending whirlwind.

An enormous thank you to my photographers: the ever wonderful and incomparable Mary Kylie Cranford, who scanned weather forecasts as anxiously as I did and rescheduled photo shoots at the drop of a hat, my brother-in-law, Dean Sickler of Dundean Studios, who stepped in at the last minute and shot pictures in the midst of making the 4th of July dinner (because it finally stopped raining long enough to take some), and Caroline Cranford who took a turn behind the camera so her big sister could take a turn in front of it. Thank you, thank you, thank you!

A million thanks must also go out to my wonderful models: Brittany Pecinich, Molly McDonough, Julia Sickler, and Mary Kylie and Caroline Cranford, who survived heat, rain, and mosquito bites – in about that order – so we could finally have pictures in this book! You are all beautiful, talented, and fabulous!

Speaking of fabulous and talented, many thank yous to my wonderful test knitters: Tracy Workman, Deborah Steiner, Linda Lemons, Sheila Perry, and my sisters Andrea Sickler and Wendy Margon. Any errors found within the covers of this book are, quite obviously, their fault!

And, of course, none of this would be possible without my long-suffering editor, Tammy Souch, who somehow manages to put up with me and doesn't get nearly enough credit for everything she does. You are the best!

And last, but not least...

This book is for my "guys" who let me be me: The Nerdling, Ceebs, "He who thinks I paint knitting," Bear, and Pippin. Major hugs, kisses, and more missed meals than you can shake a stick at. Thank goodness for restaurants!

Happy knitting everyone!

Hilary

Contents:

Secret Garden

This fabulous lacy crescent shawl is probably not for the first time knitter!

Materials:
1 skein (480 yds.) of Wolle's Color Changing Cotton or 480 yds. of any fingering weight yarn.
Size 6 40" circular needles (for c/o only)
Size 5 40" circular needles
Markers
Tapestry needle
A box of tissues and a bar of chocolate in case the cobweb lace goes wrong.

Blocked Size: 18" x 41"
Gauge: 5 sts = 1" in stockinette

The Border:

Technique:
K1tbl: Knit next stitch through the back loop.

NOTE: There are no "edge" stitches in the first section, nor are there meant to be!

With Size 6 40" circular needles, c/o 392 stitches.

Change to Size 5 40" circular needles to work pattern.

Work Rows 1 & 2 eight times
Row 1 is a Right Side Row
Row 1   P1, K1tbl, * P2, K1tbl *
Row 2   P1, * K1tbl, K1, P1 * end last repeat P2

Work Row 3 once
Row 3   P1, K1tbl, * drop next stitch off needle, P1, K1tbl *

Work Rows 4 & 5 one time
Row 4   P1, * K1tbl, P1, * end last repeat P2
Row 5   P1, K1tbl, * P1, K1tbl *

Work Row 4 once more (262 stitches)

Unravel dropped stitches all the way down to c/o edge.

The Middle:
Work Rows 11 – 20 once
Row 11 K3, * K1, yo, K1, ssk, P1, K2tog, K1, yo, P1, ssk, P1, K2tog, yo, K1, yo, * to last 4, K4
Row 12 K3, P1, * P4, K1, P1, K1, P3, K1, P4,* to last 3, K3

Row 13 K3, * K1, yo, K1, ssk, P1, K2tog, K1, P1,
       sl1 – K2tog – psso, yo, K3, yo, * to last 4, K4
Row 14 K3, P1, * P6, K1, P2, K1, P4,* to last 3, K3
Row 15 K3, *(K1, yo,)x2, ssk, P1, (K2tog)x2, yo,
       K5, yo* to last 4, K4
Row 16 K3, P1, * P7, K1, P1, K1, P5, * to last 3, K3
Row 17 K3, * K1, yo, K3, yo, sl1 – K2tog – psso, P1,
       yo, K1, ssk, P1, K2tog, K1, yo, * to last 4, K4
Row 18 K3, P1, * (P3, K1)x2, P7, * to last 3, K3
Row 19 K3, * K1, yo, K5, yo, ssk, K1, ssk, P1, K2tog,
       K1, yo, * to last 4, K4
Row 20 K3, P1, * P3, K1, P2, K1, P8, * to last 3, K3

Work Rows 11 – 14 once more

Work Rows 21 – 24 once
Row 21 K3, * (K1, yo)x2, ssk, P1, (K2tog)x2, yo, K1,
       K3tog, K1, yo, * to last 4, K4
Row 22 K3, P1, * P1, K3, (P1, K1)x2, P5, *
       to last 3, K3
Row 23 K3, * K1, yo, K3, yo, sl1 – K2tog – psso, P1,
       yo, K2tog, (P1, K1, P1) into next stitch,
       K2tog, yo, * to last 4, K4
Row 24 K3, * P2, K5, P2, K1, P5, * to last 5, P1, K4

Work Rows 25 – 28 once
Row 25 K4, * [(P1, K1,P1) into next stitch, K3tog]x3,
       (P1, K1, P1) into next stitch, K2tog, *
       to last 3, K3
Row 26 K across (277)
Row 27 K4, * [K3tog, (P1, K1, P1) into next stitch]x3,
       K3tog, * to last 4, K4
Row 28 K across (277)

The Short Row Section
Work Rows 1 – 4 once
Row 1 K145, TURN
Row 2 P14, TURN
Row 3 K13, ssk, K3, TURN
Row 4 P to 1 before last turn, P2tog, P3, TURN

Technique:
(P3tog, yo, P3tog): P3tog, leave on LHN, **yo**, purl
same 3 stitches together again.

Work Rows 5 – 20 three times
Row 5 K4, * (P3tog, yo, P3tog) K5, * to 8 before last
      turn, (P3tog, yo, P3tog), K4, ssk, K3, TURN
Row 6 P to 1 before last turn, P2tog, P3, TURN
Row 7 K to 1 before last turn, ssk, K3, TURN
Row 8 P to 1 before last turn, P2tog, P3, TURN
Row 9 K6, *(P3tog, yo, P3tog), K5, *
      to 10 before last turn, (P3tog, yo, P3tog),
      K6, ssk, K3, TURN
Row 10 P to 1 before last turn, P2tog, P3, TURN
Row 11 K to 1 before last turn, ssk, K3, TURN
Row 12 P to 1 before last turn, P2tog, P3, TURN
Row 13 K8, * (P3tog, yo, P3tog), K5, *
       to 12 before last turn, (P3tog, yo, P3tog),
       K8, ssk, K3, TURN
Row 14 P to 1 before last turn, P2tog, P3, TURN
Row 15 K to 1 before last turn, ssk, K3, TURN
Row 16 P to 1 before last turn, P2tog, P3, TURN
Row 17 K2, * (P3tog, yo, P3tog), K5, *
       to 6 before last turn, (P3tog, yo, P3tog),
       K2, ssk, K3, TURN
Row 18 P to 1 before last turn, P2tog, P3, TURN

Row 19   K to 1 before last turn, ssk, K3, TURN
Row 20   P to 1 before last turn, P2tog, P3, TURN

Work Rows 5 – 14 once more

Next row: K to 1 before last turn, ssk, K3, do NOT turn, K to end

Last row (this is a WS row): **K** to 1 before last turn, **K2tog**, K to end

b/o knitwise using the standard knitted b/o. DO NOT use a stretchy b/o.

Weave in all ends and block.

Tidal Pool

This lovely lacy crescent shawl is the epitome of versatile. Worked from the bottom up, it will be your "go to" shawl all summer!

Materials:
480 yds. Wolle's Color Changing Cotton, or 480 yds. of any fingering weight yarn.
Size 6 40" circular needles
Size 8 40" circular needles (for c/o & b/o only)
Markers
Tapestry needle

Blocked Size: 20" x 52"
Gauge: 5 sts = 1" in stockinette

The Lace Section:
Technique:
skp: sl1 – K1 – psso

All even numbered rows are worked as follows:
K3, P to last 3, K3

With Size 8 needles c/o 319 stitches.
Change to Size 6 needles to work shawl.

Work Rows 1 – 12 four times
Row 1   K3, skp, K4, yo, * K1, yo, K4,
         sl1 – K2tog – psso, K4, yo, * to last 10, K1,
         yo, K4, K2tog, K3

Row 3   K3, skp, K3, yo, K1, * K2, yo, K3,
         sl1 – K2tog – psso, K3, yo, K1, * to last 10,
         K2, yo, K3, K2tog, K3
Row 5   K3, skp, K2, yo, skp, yo, * K1, yo, K2tog, yo,
         K2, sl1 – K2tog – psso, K2, yo, skp, yo, * to
         last 10, K1, yo, K2tog, yo, K2, K2tog, K3
Row 7   K3, skp, K1, yo, skp, yo, K1, * K2, yo, K2tog,
         yo, K1, sl1 – K2tog – psso, K1, yo, skp,
         yo, K1, * to last, 10, K2, yo, K2tog, yo, K1,
         K2tog, K3
Row 9   K3, (skp, yo,)x3, * K1, (yo, K2tog,)x2, yo,
         sl1 – K2tog – psso, yo, (skp, yo,)x2, * to last
         10, K1, (yo, K2tog)x3, K3
Row 11 K3, K1, (skp, yo,)x2, K1, * K2, (yo, K2tog,)x2,
         K1, (skp, yo,)x2, K1, * to last 10, K2,
         (yo, K2tog)x2, K1, K3

Work Rows 13 & 14 one time
Row 13   K3, (K1, skp)x2, * K5, sl1 – K2tog – psso,
         K4, * (K1, K2tog,)x2, K1, K3
Row 14   K3, P to last 3, K3

The Short Row Section:
Row 1 is a RS row

Row 1   K136, TURN
Row 2   P9, TURN
Row 3   K8, ssk, K3, TURN
Row 4   P to 1 before last turn, P2tog, P3, TURN
Row 5   K to 1 before last turn, ssk, K3, TURN

Repeat Rows 4 & 5 until your last Row 4 must end, P2tog, **P2,** TURN

Next row: K to 1 before last turn, do NOT ssk, just K to end.

The Top Section:
Row 1 is a **WS** row

Technique:
K1bar: Knit the horizontal bar between the stitch you just worked and the next stitch. Do not place on LHN to work, just knit it where it is!

Work Row 1 one time
Row 1   K3, P to last 3, K3

Work Rows 2 – 5 two times
Row 2   K3, * K2tog * to last 4, K4 (work next 2
        repeats to last 3, K3)
Row 3   K3, * K1, K1bar * to last 3, K3
Row 4   K across
Row 5   K3, P to last 3, K3

Work Rows 2 – 4 once more

Knit 5 rows starting with a WS row.

Change to Size 8 needles and b/o loosely using a knitted b/o.

Weave in all ends and block.

8

Hibiscus

A garter stitch triangular shawl with a charming lace border worked in the manner favored by EZ. The increase stitches are worked in stockinette until there are enough for a new full repeat. The perfect shawl for an intermediate knit.

Materials:
435 yds. of The Twisted Knitter silky/merino, or 435 yds. of any fingering weight yarn
Size 6 circular needles
Removable markers
Tapestry needle

Blocked Size: 24" x 56"
Gauge: 5 sts = 1" in garter stitch

The Classic "Tab" start:
c/o 3
K7 rows. Do not turn after the last row is complete.
Rotate piece 90 degrees until the garter stitch edge is facing up.
pu&k 3 stitches along garter edge. Do not turn.
Rotate piece 90 degrees until the c/o edge is facing up.
pu&k 3 stitches along c/o edge. (9 stitches)

The Set Up:
Work Rows 1 & 2 once
Row 1   K3, yo, K1, yo, pm, K1, pm, yo, K1, yo, K3 (13)
Row 2   K across

The Top:
Work Rows 3 & 4 forty-one times
Row 3   K3, yo, K to m, yo, sm, K1, sm, yo, K to last 3, yo, K3
Row 4   K across
Work Row 3 once more (183)
Next Row:
K3, (kf&b)x3, K to last 5, (kf&b)x3, **K2** (189)

The Lace Edge:
Work Rows 1 & 2 once
Row 1   K3, yo, K3, pm, **K1**, * (K2tog)x2, (yo, K1)x3, **yo**, (ssk)x2, K1, * repeat to three before marker, pm, K3, yo, sm, K1, sm, yo, K3, pm, * (K2tog)x2, (yo, K1)x3, **yo**, (ssk)x2, K1, * repeat to last 7, K1, pm, K3, yo, K3 (193)
Row 2   K3, P across to last 3, K3

Work Rows 3 & 4 three times
Row 3   K3, yo, K to m, sm, K1, * (K2tog)x2, (yo, K1) x3, **yo**, (ssk)x2, K1, * to m, sm, K to center m, yo, sm, K1, sm, yo, K to m, sm, * (K2tog)x2, (yo, K1)x3, **yo**, (ssk)x2, K1, * repeat to 1 before m, K1, sm, K to last 3, yo, K3 (197)(201)(205)
Row 4   K3, P across to last 3, K3

Work Rows 5 & 6 two times
Row 5   K3, yo, K to center m, yo, sm, K1, sm,
         yo, K to last 3, yo, K3 (209)(213)
Row 6   Knit across

Repeat Rows 3 & 4 two times (217)(221)

Now comes the fun part! You now have enough additional stitches to add a pattern repeat on *both ends* of your shawl!

Work **Alternate Edge Row 3** once as follows:

Alternate Edge Row 3   K3, yo, **pm,** * (K2tog)x2, (yo, K1)x3, **yo**, (ssk) x2, K1, * once, remove marker, continue in pattern to next m, sm, K to center m, yo, sm, K1, sm, yo, K to m, sm, * (K2tog)x2, (yo, K1)x3, **yo**, (ssk)x2, K1, * repeat to m, remove m and repeat from *–* once, **pm,** yo, K3 (225)
Repeat Row 4

Guess what? On this next repeat of Row 3, you now have enough additional stitches to add a pattern repeat on *both sides* of your center stitch! BUT before you begin, you need to move your *center markers* (and your center markers only) so they are on **either side** of your center stitch.

Now comes the tricky bit. Add a **second** marker right next to the first! So in the center of your shawl you should now have 2 markers (with nothing between them), a center stitch, and 2 more markers (with nothing between them).

Now Work **Alternate Center Row 3** once as follows:

Alternate Center Row 3   K3, yo, K to m, sm, K1, * (K2tog)x2, (yo, K1)x3, **yo**, (ssk)x2, K1, * to m, slip 1st m, yo, sm, K1, sm, yo, slip 2nd m, * (K2tog)x2, (yo, K1)x3, **yo**, (ssk)x2, K1, * repeat to m, sm, K to last 3, yo, K3 (229)

Work Row 4 (Be sure when you are done with this row that you have 1 stitch *between* the markers on either side of your center stitch – these were the yo's of the row before.)

Repeat Rows 5 & 6 two times (233)(237)

Work (regular) Rows 3 & 4 four times (241)(245)(249)(253)
Work (regular) Rows 5 & 6 two times (257)(261)
Repeat (regular) Rows 3 & 4 two times (265) (269)

Guess what?! Yup, you now have enough stitches to add a pattern repeat on *both ends* of your shawl again!

Work **Alternate Edge Row 3** once (273)

Repeat Row 4

And now you have enough additional stitches to add a pattern repeat on *both sides* of your center stitch again, but 1st you need to move your center markers so they are on *both sides* of your center stitch just like before. Now add a **second** marker next to the first one again. You should now have 2 markers (with nothing between them), a center stitch, and 2 more markers (with nothing between them).

Now Work **Alternate Center Row 3** once. (277)

If you have enough yarn, repeat Row 4. If you're cutting it close, just skip to the b/o!

If you have *quite* a bit of yarn still left, work Rows 5 and 6 two more times before your b/o.

b/o knitwise using your favorite stretchy b/o, or see page 38 for the one I prefer!

Weave in all ends, block, and enjoy!

Glacier Bay

The "wind sail" shape used in this very large shawl is one of my favorites. You'll love the way it knits up and the way it drapes.

Materials :
(CC) 460 yds. of Twisted Knitter merino superwash, or 460 yds. of any fingering weight yarn.
(MC) 420 yds. of Ellyn Cooper's Yarn Sonnets Zohar's socks, or 420 yds. any fingering weight yarn.
Size 6 24" & 40" circular needles
Removable markers
Tapestry needle

Blocked Size: 26" x 68"
Gauge: 5 sts = 1" in stockinette

Note: The **MC** is also used for the lace section. Be sure to have enough yarn.

The Setup:
With **MC** c/o 1
Row 1   kf&b
Row 2   K
Row 3   K1, kf&b
Row 4   K
Row 5   K1, kf&b, K1
Row 6   K

Rows 7 – 18 make up the body of the main pattern. Work them as directed.

Work Rows 7 & 8 four times
Row 7   K1, kf&b, K to end
Row 8   K1, P to last 1, K1 (8)

Work Rows 9 & 10 two times
Row 9   K1, kf&b, K to end (10)
Row 10   K

Work Rows 11 – 18 once
Row 11   K1, kf&b, yo, ssk, * K2, yo, ssk, * end K2 (11)
Row 12   K1, P1, * P2, yo, P2tog, * end K1
Row 13   K1, kf&b, K1, yo, ssk, * K2, yo, ssk, * end K2 (12)
Row 14   K1, P1, * P2, yo, P2tog, * end P1, K1
Row 15   K1, kf&b, * K2, yo, ssk, * end K2 (13)
Row 16   K1, P1, * P2, yo, P2tog, * end P2, K1
Row 17   K1, kf&b, K1, * K2, yo, ssk, * end K2 (14)
Row 18   K1, P1, * P2, yo, P2tog, * to last 4, P2, yo, P1, K1 (15)

Work Rows 9 & 10 two times (17)

Section A Work once
Work Rows 7 & 8 five times (22)(50)
Work Rows 9 & 10 two times (24)(52)

Work Rows 15 – 18 one time (27)(55)
Work Rows 13 – 16 one time (29)(57)
Work Rows 9 & 10 two times (31)(59)
Work Rows 7 & 8 five times (36)(64)
Work Rows 9 & 10 two times (38)(66)
Work Rows 11 – 18 one time (43)(71)
Work Rows 9 & 10 two times (45)(73)

Work **Section A** once more.

Change to CC Work Rows 7 & 8 five times (78)
Change to MC :
Work Rows 9 & 10 two times
Work Rows 15 – 18 one time
Work Rows 13 – 16 one time
Work Rows 9 & 10 two times (87)
Change to CC Work Rows 7 & 8 five times (92)
Change to MC:
Work Rows 9 & 10 two times
Work Rows 11 – 18 one time
Work Rows 9 & 10 two times (101)
Change to CC Work Rows 7 & 8 five times
Change to MC :
Work Rows 9 & 10 two times
Work Rows 15 – 18 one time
Work Rows 13 – 16 one time
Work Rows 9 & 10 two times
Cut MC

Section B Work once
Change to CC :
Work Rows 7 & 8   five times (120)(148)
Work Rows 9 & 10 two times
Work Rows 11 – 18 one time (127)(155)

Work Rows 9 & 10 two times
Work Rows 7 & 8 five times (134)(162)
Work Rows 9 & 10 two times
Work Rows 15 – 18 one time (139)(167)
Work Rows 13 – 16 one time
Work Rows 9 & 10 two times (143)(171)

Work **Section B** once more.

After second repeat of **Section B**, work Rows 7 & 8 five times (176)
Then work Rows 9 & 10 two times (178)
Cut CC

Section C – The Lace Edge
Change to MC:
Row 1   Knit
You should now have 178 stitches. Take the time to count and adjust if necessary.
pm at the end of the row, pu&k 1 stitch in the corner, **pm.**
Rotate work 90 degrees. The straight edge, not the increase edge, should now be facing up.

Starting with the topmost garter ridge, count off 15 garter ridge bumps and **pm**. Continue counting off 15 garter ridge bumps and pms all the way down the edge.
pu&k 178 stitches along the straight edge
AS FOLLOWS:
In 1st marked off section pu&k 17, (pick up stitches in the garter bumps, not between them, where possible), pu&k 16 in each of the next 9 sections, pu&k 17 in the last section, pu&k 1 in c/o stitch.

You should now have: 178 stitches along the top edge, a marker, one corner stitch, a marker, and 178 stitches along the vertical edge. Remove all *edge* markers, but **DO NOT** remove the markers on either side of your corner stitch. **Please take the time to count your stitches.**

The Border:
Row 2 is a WS row
Work Row 2 once
Row 2   K to m, yo, sm, **P1**, sm, yo, K to end

Work Rows 3 – 6 six times.
Row 3   K2, * yo, K2tog, * to 1 before m, K1, yo, sm, K1, sm, yo, K1 * K2tog, yo, * to last 2, K2
Row 4   K2, P to last 2, K2
Row 5   K3, * ssk, yo, * (be careful not to lose this yo!) repeat to 1 before m, K1, yo, sm, K1, sm, yo, K1, * yo, ssk, * to last 3, K3
Row 6   K2, P to last 2, K2
Cut MC

The Edge:
With CC:
Work Rows 1 & 2 two times
Row 1   K to m, yo, sm, K1, sm, yo, K to end
Row 2   K

Work Row 1 once more, then b/o knitwise using the standard knitted b/o, not a stretchy one.

Weave in all ends and block.

Rose Trellis

Worked from the top down, this fabulous, graceful, three triangle shawl will quickly become one of your favorites, as it truly stays in place.

Materials:
480 yds. of Wolle's Color Changing Cotton, or 480 yds. of any fingering weight yarn.
Size 6 40" circular needles
Markers
Tapestry needle

Blocked Size: 15" x 40"
Gauge: 5 sts = 1" in stockinette

Technique:
M1R: with LHN pick up horizontal bar between stitch just worked and next stitch from **back to front,** K into front.
M1L: with LHN pick up horizontal bar between stitch just worked and next stitch from **front to back**, K into back.

c/o 3
K 11 rows, do not turn after last row. Rotate 90 degrees so garter edge is facing up.
pu&k 5 along garter edge. Do not turn, rotate 90 degrees so c/o edge is facing up.
pu&k 3 along c/o edge. (11)

The Set Up:
Work Rows 1 – 4 one time
Row 1   K3, pm, (M1R, K1, M1L, pm, K1, pm,)x2, M1R, K1, M1L, pm, K3
Row 2   K3, P to last 3, K3
Row 3   K3, sm, (M1R, K to m, M1L, sm, K1, sm,)x2, M1R, K to m, M1L, sm, K3
Row 4   K3, P to last 3, K3

Repeat Rows 3 & 4 until there are 53 stitches in each of the three triangle sections. (167)

The Lace Pattern:
Technique:
sl1 – K2tog – psso: slip one, knit the next 2 stitches together, then pass the slipped stitch over the K2tog.

All even numbered rows are worked as follows:
K3, P to last 3, K3

Work Rows 1 – 10 one time.

Row 1   K3, sm, [M1R, K2tog, yo, K1, *yo, ssk, K7, K2tog, yo, K1, * to last 2, yo, ssk, M1L, **sm, K1, sm**]x3, working 3rd repeat to last 5, yo, ssk, M1L, sm, K3

Row 3 K3, sm, [M1R, K2tog, yo, K2, * K1, yo, ssk, K5, K2tog, yo, K2, * to last 3, K1, yo, ssk, M1L, sm, K1, sm] x3, working 3rd repeat to last 6, K1, yo, ssk, M1L, sm, K3

Row 5 K3, sm, [M1R, (K2tog, yo,)x2, K1, *(yo, ssk)x2, K3, (K2tog, yo,)x2, K1, * to last 4, (yo, ssk,)x2, M1L, sm, K1, sm]x3, work 3rd repeat to last 7, (yo, ssk,)x2, M1L, sm, K3

Row 7 K3, sm, [M1R, (K2tog, yo,)x2, K2, * K1, (yo, ssk,)x2, K1, (K2tog, yo,)x2, K2, * to last 5, K1, (yo, ssk)x2, M1L, sm, K1, sm]x3, work 3rd repeat to last 8, K1, (yo, ssk)x2, M1L, sm, K3

Row 9 K3, sm, [M1R, (K2tog, yo)x3, K1, * (yo, ssk)x2, yo, sl1 – K2tog – psso, yo, (K2tog, yo)x2, K1,* to last 6, (yo, ssk,)x3, M1L, sm, K1, sm]x3, work 3rd repeat to last 9, (yo, ssk,)x3, M1L, sm, K3

Work Rows 11 – 20 six times

Row 11 K3, sm, [M1R, **K1,** yo, K1, * (yo, ssk,)x2, yo, sl1 – K2tog – psso, yo, (K2tog, yo,)x2, K1, * to last 1, yo, K1, M1L, sm, K1, sm]x3, work 3rd repeat to last 4, yo, K1, M1L, sm, K3

Row 13 K3, sm, [M1R, K2tog, yo, K2, * K1, (yo, ssk)x2, K1, (K2tog, yo,)x2, K2,* to last 3, K1, yo, ssk, M1L, sm, K1, sm]x3, work 3rd repeat to last 6, K1, yo, ssk, M1L, sm, K3

Row 15 K3, sm, [M1R, (K2tog, yo,)x2, K1, * (yo, ssk)x2, yo, sl1 – K2tog – psso, yo, (K2tog, yo,)x2, K1, * to last 4, (yo, ssk,)x2, M1L, sm, K1, sm]x3, work 3rd repeat to last 7, (yo, ssk,)x2, M1L, sm, K3

Row 17 K3, sm, [M1R, (K2tog, yo,)x2, K2, * K1, (yo, ssk,)x2, K1, (K2tog, yo,)x2, K2,* to last 5, K1, (yo, ssk)x2, M1L, sm, K1, sm]x3, work 3rd repeat to last 8, K1, (yo, ssk)x2, M1L, sm, K3

Row 19 K3, sm, [M1R, (K2tog, yo,)x3, K1, * (yo, ssk)x2, yo, sl1 – K2tog – psso, yo, (K2tog, yo,)x2, K1 * to last 6, (yo, K2tog,)x3, M1L, sm, K1, sm]x3, work 3rd repeat to last 9, (yo, K2tog,)x3, M1L, sm, K3

Next Row, b/o using stretchy b/o (see page 38).

If you'd like to make the shawl longer, work Rows 11 – 20 to desired length.

Weave in all ends and block thoroughly.

Emerald Isle

I absolutely adore these sail-shaped shawls. The main body of this one is worked in garter stitch with the lace border added after using a clever little trick!

Materials:
(MC) 1 55 gram skein of Wolle's Color Changing Cotton, or 240 yds. of any fingering weight yarn in either a tonal or variegated colorway.
(CC) 1 55 gram skein of Wolle's solid cotton, or 240 yds. of any fingering weight yarn in a solid color.
Size 6 24" & 40" circular needles
Size 8 needles (can be straight or dpn) for b/o only
1 **removable** marker
Tapestry needle

Blocked Size: 24" x 58"
Gauge: 6 sts = 1" in garter stitch

The Shawl Body:
Hint: Odd rows are RS rows.
Place a removable marker **through** your fabric on the Right Side (RS) so you don't forget which side is which!

With **MC** and Size 6 24" circular needle:
c/o 1
Row 1   kf&b
Row 2   K
Row 3   K1, kf&b
Row 4   K

Row 5   K1, kf&b, K to end
Row 6   K

Repeat Rows 5 & 6 until you have 119 stitches. If you are in danger of running out of your MC before you have 119 stitches, **on the last Repeat of Row 5 that you *can* work**, cast on any extra stitches you need to reach the 119 using the Cable Cast On Method at the **beginning of the row** (see pg. 38). Be sure to work one last repeat of Row 6 before dropping your MC.

The rest of the shawl is worked entirely with your CC.

With **CC** and Size 6 40" circular needle:
K one row, pm (119)
It's very important that you place a marker here so you know where your "corner" is later!
You should now be at the perpendicular corner of your shawl, and all your stitches should be on your 40" needle.

Rotate work 90 degrees so the perpendicular garter stitch edge is now facing up. Be absolutely sure this is the edge that forms the right angle with your live stitches and is not the "increase" edge.

22

The Edge:

You're now going to p/u & k stitches from your garter edge, but **NOT** in the traditional manner! In the traditional manner, you would pick up the "bumps" along the edge, but that won't work here, so instead you're going to be picking up the **straight thread** between the bumps as follows:

With LHN p/u straight thread between garter bumps from front to back and **Ktbl.** Pick up ONLY the outermost leg of the strand, not both strands.

Working down the perpendicular edge p/u&ktbl **117 stitches.** (Be sure to knit the picked up thread **through the back loop**!) Pick up 1 more stitch by working into the c/o bump.

You should now have 119 stitches along the top edge, a marker, and 118 stitches along the side edge.

Note: The side lace border is a knitted on edge that is worked by casting on extra stitches that are then joined to the main body of the shawl on WS Rows 1 & 3 with a P2tog (1 edge stitch and 1 lace stitch) binding off the side of your shawl as you work it.

Side Lace Border Set Up:

Turn work so WS is facing and cast on 22 stitches using the Cable Cast On Method. (see pg. 38)
Now work Row 3 of **Side Lace Pattern** back towards the body of the shawl. (This is a WS row)
Then work Row 4 of **Side Lace Pattern** once.

Side Lace Pattern:
Technique:

Sl2–K1–p2sso: Slip the next two stitches **knitwise with yarn in back**, knit one, then pass the two slipped stitches over the knit one and off.

Row 1   K1, P20, P2tog, TURN
Row 2   **K1**, * (yo, ssk)x2, K1, (K2tog, yo)x2, K1, * end last repeat K2, TURN
Row 3   K1, P20, P2tog, TURN
Row 4   **K2,** * yo, ssk, yo, sl2–K1–p2sso, yo, K2tog, yo, K3, * TURN

Now work Rows 1 – 4 of **Side Lace Pattern** until you have worked all your edge stitches. How do you know when you're there? You will have just finished a Row 4 and working row 1 once more would necessitate moving the "corner" marker.

Once you have worked all your edge stitches, stop. You should have 22 lace stitches, a marker, then 119 stitches.

Please be sure you have the right number of stitches before continuing.

Work next row as follows (this is a WS row):
K1, P20, P2tog (removing marker as you come to it), **KNIT** to last 3, (kf&b)x2, K1 (143 stitches)

Work Rows 2 – 4 of **Top Lace Pattern** once.
Row 2 is a Right Side Row.

Top Lace Pattern:

Row 1   K1, P to last 1, K1

Row 2   K2, * (yo, ssk)x2, K1, (K2tog, yo)x2, K1, *
            end last repeat K2

Row 3   K1, P to last 1, K1

Row 4   K2, * K1, yo, ssk, yo, sl2-K1-p2sso, yo,
            K2tog, yo, K2, * end last repeat K3

Now work rows 1 – 4 of **Top Lace Pattern** until top lace edge is the same height/width as the lace on the perpendicular edge.

With Size 8 needles, b/o purlwise loosely. Do not use a stretchy b/o, as the lace pattern is not intended to "flare" outwards.

Block lightly and enjoy!

24

Garden Gate

This "Baktus" style shawl is a must have for your wardrobe! Worked from end to end, the body and lace edge are worked at the same time, so once you're done, you're done!

Materials:
400 yds. Unplanned Peacock Twisty sock yarn, or 400 yds. of any fingering weight yarn.
Size 6 24" circular needles
Markers
Tapestry needle

Unblocked Size: 10" x 66"
Unblocked Gauge: 7 sts = 1" in garter stitch

c/o 22
Knit one row

The Beginning & The End:
Row 1 is a Wrong Side Row

On the first repeat of Row 1 place a marker where it says "sm."

Work Rows 1 – 10 five times
Row 1   sl1, K2, yo, K2tog, **sm,** K1, (yo, K2tog)x7, yo, K2 (22)
Row 2   K to m, sm, K2, yo, K2tog, K1 (23)
Row 3   sl1, K2, yo, K2tog, sm, K4, (yo, K2tog)x6, yo, K2 (24)
Row 4   K to m, sm, K2, yo, K2tog, K1 (24)

Row 5   sl1, K2, yo, K2tog, sm, K7, (yo, K2tog)x5, yo, K2 (25)
Row 6   K to m, sm, K2, yo, K2tog, K1 (25)
Row 7   sl1, K2, yo, K2tog, sm, K10, (yo, K2tog)x4, yo, K2 (26)
Row 8   K to m, sm, K2, yo, K2tog, K1 (26)
Row 9   sl1, K2, yo, K2tog, sm, K21 (26)
Row 10 b/o 4, K to m, sm, K2, yo, K2tog, K1 (22)

(Stitch count is for first repeat only.)

Work Rows **1 – 9** of **The Beginning & The End** once more

Work next row as follows:
b/o 4, K15, kf&b, K2, yo, K2tog, K1, removing the marker as you come to it. (23)

Increase Section #1:
Work **first repeat** of Row 1 as follows:
sl1, K2, yo, K2tog, **pm**, kf&b, **pm**, K1, (yo, K2tog)x7, yo, K2 (This is a WS row)

Work Rows 2 – 10 of **Increase Section #1** once
Work Rows 1 – 10 of **Increase Section #1** nine times

Row 1 sl1, K2, yo, K2tog, **sm,** K to 1 before next m, kf&b, **sm,** K1, (yo, K2tog)x7, yo, K2
Row 2 (K to m, sm,)x2, K2, yo, K2tog, K1
Row 3 sl1, K2, yo, K2tog, sm, K to m, sm, K4, (yo, K2tog)x6, yo, K2
Row 4 (K to m, sm,)x2 K2, yo, K2tog, K1
Row 5 sl1, K2, yo, K2tog, sm, K to m, sm, K7, (yo, K2tog)x5, yo, K2
Row 6 (K to m, sm,)x2, K2, yo, K2tog, K1
Row 7 sl1, K2, yo, K2tog, sm, K to m, sm, K10, (yo, K2tog)x4, yo, K2
Row 8 (K to m, sm,)x2, K2, yo, K2tog, K1
Row 9 sl1, K2, yo, K2tog, sm, K to m, sm, K21
Row 10 b/o 4, (K to m, sm,)x2, K2, yo, K2tog, K1

Increase Section #2:
Work Rows 1 – 10 ten times
Row 1 sl1, K2, yo, K2tog, sm, K to 1 before next m, kf&b, sm, K1, (yo, K2tog)x7, yo, K2
Row 2 (K to m, sm,)x2, K2, yo, K2tog, K1
Row 3 sl1, K2, yo, K2tog, sm, K to m, sm, K4, (yo, K2tog)x6, yo, K2
Row 4 (K to m, sm,)x2 K2, yo, K2tog, K1
Row 5 sl1, K2, yo, K2tog, sm, K to m, sm, K7, (yo, K2tog)x5, yo, K2

Row 6 K to m, sm, **kf&b,** K to m, sm, K2, yo, K2tog, K1
Row 7 sl1, K2, yo, K2tog, sm, K to m, sm, K10, (yo, K2tog)x4, yo, K2
Row 8 (K to m, sm,)x2, K2, yo, K2tog, K1
Row 9 sl1, K2, yo, K2tog, sm, K to m, sm, K21
Row 10 b/o 4, (K to m, sm,)x2, K2, yo, K2tog, K1

Center Section: There are no increases in this section.
Work Rows 1 – 10 two times
Row 1 sl1, K2, yo, K2tog, sm, **K to m,** sm, K1, (yo, K2tog)x7, yo, K2
Row 2 (K to m, sm,)x2, K2, yo, K2tog, K1
Row 3 sl1, K2, yo, K2tog, sm, K to m, sm, K4, (yo, K2tog)x6, yo, K2
Row 4 (K to m, sm,)x2 K2, yo, K2tog, K1
Row 5 sl1, K2, yo, K2tog, sm, K to m, sm, K7, (yo, K2tog)x5, yo, K2
Row 6 (K to m, sm,)x2, K2, yo, K2tog, K1
Row 7 sl1, K2, yo, K2tog, sm, K to m, sm, K10, (yo, K2tog)x4, yo, K2
Row 8 (K to m, sm,)x2, K2, yo, K2tog, K1
Row 9 sl1, K2, yo, K2tog, sm, K to m, sm, K21
Row 10 b/o 4, (K to m, sm,)x2, K2, yo, K2tog, K1

Decrease Section #1:
Work Rows 1 – 10 ten times
Row 1 sl1, K2, yo, K2tog, sm, K to 2 before next m, **ssk,** sm, K1, (yo, K2tog)x7, yo, K2
Row 2 (K to m, sm,)x2, K2, yo, K2tog, K1
Row 3 sl1, K2, yo, K2tog, sm, K to m, sm, K4, (yo, K2tog)x6, yo, K2
Row 4 (K to m, sm)x2, K2, yo, K2tog, K1

Row 5 sl1, K2, yo, K2tog, sm, K to m, sm, K7,
(yo, K2tog)x5, yo, K2

Row 6 K to m, sm, **K2tog**, K to m, sm, K2, yo,
K2tog, K1

Row 7 sl1, K2, yo, K2tog, sm, K to m, sm, K10,
(yo, K2tog)x4, yo, K2

Row 8 (K to m, sm,)x2, K2, yo, K2tog, K1

Row 9 sl1, K2, yo, K2tog, sm, K to m, sm, K21

Row 10 b/o 4, (K to m, sm,)x2, K2, yo, K2tog, K1

Decrease Section #2:

Work Rows 1 – 10 **nine times**

Row 1 sl1, K2, yo, K2tog, sm, K to 2 before next m,
ssk, sm, K1, (yo, K2tog)x7, yo, K2

Row 2 (K to m, sm,)x2, K2, yo, K2tog, K1

Row 3 sl1, K2, yo, K2tog, sm, K to m, sm, K4,
(yo, K2tog)x6, yo, K2

Row 4 (K to m, sm,)x2 K2, yo, K2tog, K1

Row 5 sl1, K2, yo, K2tog, sm, K to m, sm, K7,
(yo, K2tog)x5, yo, K2

Row 6 (K to m, sm,)x2, K2, yo, K2tog, K1

Row 7 sl1, K2, yo, K2tog, sm, K to m, sm, K10,
(yo, K2tog)x4, yo, K2

Row 8 (K to m, sm,)x2, K2, yo, K2tog, K1

Row 9 sl1, K2, yo, K2tog, sm, K to m, sm, K21

Row 10 b/o 4, (K to m, sm,)x2, K2, yo, K2tog, K1

Work Rows **1 – 9** of **Decrease Section #2** once more

Work next row as follows:
b/o 4, K15, ssk, K2, yo, K2tog, K1

The Beginning & The End Reprise:

Row 1 is a Wrong Side row

Work 1st repeat of Row 1 as follows:

Row 1 sl1, K2, yo, K2tog, sm, slip next stitch to RHN,
remove marker, place slipped stitch back on
LHN, ssk, K1, (yo, K2tog)x7, yo, K2

Work Rows 2 – 10 of The Beginning & The End once
Work Rows 1 – 10 of The Beginning & The End four
times.

b/o all stitches on the last repeat of Row 10.

Smooth Sailing

This is a heart-shaped shawl worked from the top down. It starts with the ever popular "tab" and uses increases on right and wrong side rows to form it's unusual shape. It's a very fast, fun knit full of different pattern stitches.

Materials:
2 skeins Queensland Brumbay, 216 yds. each, or 432 yds. of fingering weight yarn.
Size 7 24" & 40" circular needles
Markers
Tapestry needle

Blocked Size: 36" x 84"
Gauge: 5 sts = 1" in stockinette

Technique:
M1R: With LHN pick up horizontal bar between stitch just worked and next stitch from **back to front,** K into front.
M1L: With LHN pick up horizontal bar between stitch just worked and next stitch from **front to back,** K into back.

The classic "tab" cast on:
c/o 3
K 11 rows, do not turn after last row. Rotate 90 degrees so garter edge is facing up.
pu&k 5 along garter edge. Do not turn, rotate 90 degrees so c/o edge is facing up.
pu&k 3 along c/o edge. (11)

Work next row as follows: (this is a **WS row**):
K3, yo, P2, pm, P1, pm, P1, yo, K3 (13 stitches)

Section 1 (stockinette)
Work Rows 1 & 2 three times
Row1   K3, yo, K to m, M1R, sm, K1, sm, M1L, K to last 3, yo, K3 (17)(23)(29)
Row 2   K3, yo, P to last 3, yo, K3 (19)(25)(31)

Section 2 (not a garter ridge)
Row 1 **is a RS Row**

Work Rows 1 – 4 four times
Row 1   K3, yo, **P** to m, **wyib** M1R, sm, **K1**, sm, M1L, **P** to last 3, yo, K3
Row 2   K3, yo, **P** to last 3, yo, K3 (37)(49)(61)(73)
Row 3   K3, yo, K to m, M1R, sm, K1, sm, M1L, K to last 3, yo , K3
Row 4   K3, yo, P to last 3, yo K3 (43)(55)(67)(79)

Section 3 (triple knot)
Technique:
MK: K3tog, leave on LHN, K1st stitch again then K 2nd & 3rd stitches together.

Work Rows 1 – 4 four times
Row1   K3, yo, K to m, M1R, sm, K1, sm, M1L, K to last 3, yo, K3
Row 2   K3, yo, **K** to last 3, yo, K3 **(Purl the center stitch)** (85)(97)(109)(121)(133)
Row 3   K3, yo, * MK * to m, M1R, sm, K1, sm, M1L, * MK * to last 3, yo, K3
Row 4   K3, yo, P to last 3, yo, K3 (91)(103)(115)(127)
After 4th repeat, work Rows 1 & 2 once more

Section 4 (stockinette)
Work Rows 1 & 2 one time
Row1   K3, yo, K to m, M1R, sm, K1, sm, M1L, K to last 3, yo, K3 (137)
Row 2   K3, yo, P to last 3, yo, K3 (139)

Section 5 (crossed grain)
Hint: the P1tbl is worked through the "yo" of the previous row, except for the first repeat. The P1tbl will twist the stitch. This is important!

Work Rows 1 – 4 three times
Row1   K3, yo, K to m, M1R, sm, K1, sm, M1L, K to last 3, yo, K3
Row 2   K3, yo, P to last 3, yo, K3 (145)(157)(169)
Row 3   K3, yo, K1, * (**P2tog**, yo) * to m (don't lose the last yo!), M1R, sm, K1, sm, M1L, * (yo, P2tog) * to last 4, K1, yo, K3

Row 4   K3, yo, K1, * (P1tbl, P1) * to m, sm, K1, sm, * (P1, P1tbl) * to last 4, K1, yo, K3 (151)(163)(175)

Section 6 (stockinette)
Work Rows 1 & 2 one time
Row1   K3, yo, K to m, M1R, sm, K1, sm, M1L, K to last 3, yo, K3 (179)
Row 2   K3, yo, P to last 3, yo, K3 (181)

Section 7 (fancy garter)
Work Rows 1 – 4 four times

Row 1   K3, yo, K to m, M1R, sm, K1, sm, M1L, K to last 3, yo K3 (185)(197)(209) (221)
Row 2   K3, yo, K1, * **K2tog**, * to m, sm, **P1**, sm, * **K2tog**, * to last 4, K1, yo, K3
Row 3   K3, yo, K2, * kf&b * to m, M1R, sm, K1, sm, M1L, * kf&b * to last 5, K2, yo, K3 (191)(203)(215)(227)
Row 4   K3, yo, P to last 3, yo, K3

Section 8 (garter)
Work Rows 1 & 2 one time
Row 1   K3, yo, K to m, M1R, sm, K1, sm, M1L, K to last 3, yo, K3 (233)
Row 2   K3, yo, **K** to last 3, yo, K3

Section 9 (stockinette)
Work Rows 1 & 2 two times
Row 1   K3, yo, K to m, M1R, sm, K1, sm, M1L, K to last 3, yo, K3 (239)(245)
Row 2   K3, yo, P to last 3, yo, K3

Section 10 (Coral stitch)
Technique:
K1bar: Knit the horizontal bar between the stitch you just worked and the next stitch. Do not place on LHN to work, just knit it where it is!

Work Rows 1 – 12 once
Row 1 K3, yo, * K2tog * to m, M1R, sm, K1, sm, M1L, * K2tog * to last 3, yo, K3 (131)(149)
Row 2 K3, yo, K1, * K1, K1bar, * to 1 before m, K1, sm, **P1**, sm, K1, * K1bar, K1 * to last 4, K1, yo, K3 (253)(289)
Row 3 K3, yo, K to m, M1R, sm, K1, sm, M1L, K to last 3, yo, K3 (257)(293)
Row 4 K3, yo, P to last 3, yo, K3
Row 5 K3, yo, K to m, M1R, sm, K1, sm, M1L, K to last 3, yo, K3
Row 6 K3, yo, P to last 3, yo, K3 (265)(301)
Row 7 K3, yo, K1, * K2tog * to m, M1R, sm, K1, sm, M1L, * K2tog * to last 4, K1 yo, K3 (140)
Row 8 K3, yo, K2, * K1, K1bar, * to 1 before m, K1, sm, **P1**, sm, K1, * K1bar, K1 * to last 5, K2, yo, K3 (271)
Row 9 K3, yo, K to m, M1R, sm, K1, sm, M1L, K to last 3, yo, K3 (275)
Row 10 K3, yo, P to last 3, yo, K3
Row 11 K3, yo, K to m, M1R, sm, K1, sm, M1L, K to last 3, yo, K3 (281)
Row 12 K3, yo, P to last 3, yo, K3   (283)
Work Rows 1 – 6 once more

Section 11 (garter)
Work Rows 1 & 2 five times
Row 1 K3, yo, K to m, M1R, sm, K1, sm, M1L, K to last 3, yo, K3
Row 2 K3, yo, **K** to last 3, yo, K3

Bind off using your favorite stretchy b/o. Don't have one? See page 38!

Block thoroughly, this yarn really stretches!

Castaway

A delightful open and airy half-Pi shawl worked in the traditional manner.
A knitted-on border does double duty as the bind off.

Materials:
(MC) 1 skein Unplanned Peacock Twisty sock yarn, 400 yds., or 400 yds. of any fingering weight yarn.
(CC) 1 skein Malabrigo Arroyo, or 175 yds. of any fingering weight yarn.
Size 7 24" & 40" circular needles
Markers
Tapestry needle

Blocked Size: 20" x 46"
Gauge: 6 sts = 1" in stockinette

Note:
As you change colors, you can carry them up the sides or cut them, either way works fine.

The Set Up:
With **MC**
c/o 3
Knit 13 rows do not turn at end of last row. Rotate work 90 degrees so garter edge is facing up.
pu&k6 along garter edge. Do not turn at end of last row. Rotate work 90 degrees so c/o edge is facing up, pu&k3. (12)

Row 1 is a WS row.
Work Set Up Rows 1 & 2 once.
Row 1 K3, P6, K3
Row 2 K3, yo, kf&b, (yo, K2)x2, yo kf&b, yo, K3 (19)

Section 1:
Row 1 is a WS row.
Work Rows 1 – 16 of **Section 1** one time.
Still with **MC**:
Row 1 K3, P to last 3, K3

With **CC**:
Row 2 K across
Row 3 K across
Row 4 K3, (yo, K1) to last 3, yo, K3 (33)(117)
Row 5 K across

With **MC**:
Row 6 K across
Row 7 K3, P to last 3, K3
Row 8 K across
Row 9 K3, P to last 3, K3

With **CC**:
Row 10 K across
Row 11 K across

Row 12   K3, (yo, K1) to last 3, yo, K3 (61)(229)
Row 13   K across

With **MC:**
Row 14   K across
Row 15   K3, P to last 3, K3
Row 16   K across

Work Rows **1 – 7** of **Section 1** once more, changing colors as directed.

Section 2:
Technique:
RT: K2tog, leave on LHN, K 1st stitch again
LT: Skip 1st stitch, knit 2nd stitch **tbl**, then knit the 1st & 2nd stitches together **tbl**

Row 1 is a RS row
Work Rows 1 – 4 of **Section 2** four times still using **MC**.
Row 1   K4, (yo, RT) to last 3, K3
Row 2   K3, P1, (P2tog, P1) to last 3, K3
Row 3   K3, LT, (yo, LT) to last 4, K4
Row 4   K3, P2, (P2tog, P1) to last 4, P1, K3

Go back to **Section 1** and work Rows **10 – 15** once more, changing colors as directed.

Section 3:
Work Rows 1 – 8 of **Section 3** once, changing colors as directed.

With **MC**
Row 1   K across

Row 2   K3, P to last 3, K3

With **CC**
Row 3   K across
Row 4   K across
Row 5   K3, (yo, K2tog) to last 4, yo, K1, yo, K3 (231)(233)(235)
Row 6   K across

With **MC**
Row 7   K across
Row 8   K3, P to last 3, K3

Work Rows 1 – 4 of **Section 2** four times, still with **MC**.
Work Rows 3 – 8 of **Section 3** once more, changing colors as directed.
Work Rows 1 – 6 of **Section 3** once more, changing colors as directed.

With **MC**
Work next 2 Rows once
Row 1   K3, K2tog, K to last 5, K2tog, K3   (233)
Row 2   K3, P to last 3, K3, removing any markers you may have placed as you come to them.

TURN, still with **MC**, c/o 4 using the Cable Cast On Method on page 38.

STOP! Please be sure to take the time to count your stitches now. You should have 237 stitches. Adjust if necessary.

Note: The Border is a knitted on edge that binds off the shawl as it is worked by knitting one stitch from the shawl with one stitch from the Border pattern on every even numbered row.

The Border is worked completely in your **MC**.

Technique:
00: this is a double yo

Work next row as follows:
K3, K2tog (1 edge stitch & 1 border stitch), TURN

Now work Rows 1 – 8 of **The Border** 59 times.
On last row 8, b/o all stitches.

The Border:
Row 1   K1, 00, K2tog, K1, TURN
Row 2   K3, P1, K2tog, TURN
Row 3   K3, 00, K2, TURN
Row 4   K3, P1, K2, K2tog, TURN
Row 5   K1, 00, K2tog, K4, TURN
Row 6   K6, P1, K2tog, TURN
Row 7   K8, TURN
Row 8   b/o 4, K2, K2tog, TURN

Weave in all ends, block, and enjoy!

Abbreviations:

c/o – cast on
b/o – bind off
pm – place marker
sm – slip marker
RHN – Right hand needle
LHN – Left hand needle
RS – right side row
WS – wrong side row
K – knit
P – Purl
yo – yarn over
K2tog – Knit the next 2 stitches together.
P2tog – Purl the next 2 stitches together.
K3tog – Knit the next 3 stitches together.
P3tog – Purl the next 3 stitches together.
ssk – Slip the next 2 stitches knitwise to RHN. Return to LHN and knit them together.
tbl – Knit or purl through the **back** loop as directed.
skp (slip1 – k1 – psso) – (see Techniques)
M1R – Make one to the right. (see Techniques)
M1L – Make one to the left. (see Techniques)
kf&b – Knit into the front and the back of the next stitch. 1 new stitch made.
pu&k – Pick up a stitch as directed and knit into it at the same time. 1 new stitch made.
sl1 – Slip the next stitch. Unless directed otherwise, slip the stitch purlwise wyib.
wyib – with yarn in back
wyif – with yarn in front
00 – double yo
TURN – Turn your work now without working the remainder of the stitches still on your needle, and
        begin working back the other way as directed.

Techniques:

skp (sl1 – K1 – psso): Slip the next stitch purlwise wyib to RHN, knit 1, then pass the slipped stitch over the knitted stitch and off the needle.

sl1 – K2tog – psso: Slip the next stitch purlwise wyib to RHN, knit the next 2 stitch together, pass the slipped stitch over the K2tog, and off the needle.

sl2 – K1 – p2sso: Slip the next 2 stitches **knitwise** wyib to RHN, knit 1, passed the 2 slipped stitches over the K1 and off the needle

RT: K2tog, leave on LHN, Knit 1st stitch again

LT: Skip 1st stitch, Knit 2nd stitch **tbl**, leave on LHN, then Knit 1st & 2nd stitches together **tbl**

00: Wrap yarn around needle two times.

M1R: With LHN pick up horizontal bar between stitch just worked and next stitch from **back to front,** Knit into the front of it. 1 new stitch made.

M1L: With LHN pick up horizontal bar between stitch just worked and next stitch from **front to back,** Knit into the back of it. 1 new stitch made.

MK: Knit the next 3 stitch together, leave on LHN, Knit 1st stitch again, then knit the 2nd & 3rd stitches together.

K1bar: Knit the horizontal bar between the stitch just worked and the next stitch. Do not place on LHN needle first, just knit it where it is.

(P3tog, yo, P3tog): Purl the next 3 stitches together, leave on LHN, make a yo, then purl the same 3 stitches together again.

(P1, K1, P1): This is the same as Pfb&f. Purl into the front, the back and the front again of the next stitch. 2 new stitches made.

Cable Cast On Method:

* Insert RHN *between* last 2 stitches on LHN, wrap yarn around tip and pull loop through. Place loop on LHN * 1 stitch made. Repeat.

The Stretchy Bind Off:

K2, pass the first stitch over the second and off, *yo, pass the knit stitch over the yo and off, K1, pass the yo over the knit stitch and off* repeat to last stitch. Cut yarn, make yo, pass last stitch over yo and pull thread through.

Tips and Tricks:

Here are some helpful bits of information that will help you successfully knit the patterns in this book (without pulling your hair out, hopefully).

- Repeats are shown between * asterisks *.
- Run "life lines" often.
- Use markers. Lots of markers!
- Drink heavily.
- If there is any errata, it can be found on Ravelry or the Amazon.com description for this book.

Resources:

All the yarns used in these patterns (except for the Queensland Brumbay) are from the workshops of local indie dyers whose yarns I just can't resist! There is nothing better than going to a yarn event and spending time with each and every one of them, browsing through their wares, and finding that one skein (or half a dozen) you just have to go home with!

Wolle's Yarn Creations
Elizabeth Drumm
Wollesyarncreations.etsy.com
on Ravelry at: ravelry.com/groups/fans-of-wolles-yarn-creations
Wollesyarncreations@gmail.com

Unplanned Peacock Studio
Natasha Laity Snyder
www.unplannedpeacock.com
on Ravelry at: ravelry.com/groups/unplanned-peacock

The Twisted Knitter
Kim Pate
109 North 3rd Street
Mebane, NC 27302
919-563-2468
kim@thetwistedknitter.com

Ellyn Cooper's Yarn Sonnets
Ellyn Cooper
135 Hanover-Versailles Road
Sprague, CT 06330
860-822-0829
ellyncoopersyarnsonnets.net

Queensland Yarns
Available at your LYS or through online yarn stores such as:
WEBS, Jimmy Bean, Paradisefibers, Knittingfever, etc.

About the Designer:

Ummm... uh... well, at various times in my life, I've been a successful author, artist, and knitting designer...
I'm plump, which is different than being over weight... I'm completely crazy...
Okay this is NOT going well... What the heck am I supposed to say?!!

Never mind, let me take it from here...
How about, Hilary learned to knit when she was four. A very nice lady by the name of Mrs. Montkowski
taught her.

Excuse me, but she was *not* a nice lady. She was large and scary, and wore the most dreadful brown tweed
suits, and had hair on her chin – you remember these things when you're small, you know...

As I was saying... that was when she learned to knit. However, she soon exchanged two sharp pointy
sticks for one – namely a pencil –and became a published author at the age of nine. Writing gave way to
painting-

No it didn't!

Would you please be quiet and let me finish this?
Now where was I? Oh yes, and between college, marriage, dogs, and babies, she has had a very long ca-
reer doing arty design things while painting and scribbling stories, collecting along the way some very
strange fans of her writing-

Well, let's face it, the writing is also quite strange!!!

...and a more respectable audience for her paintings, several of which hang in fairly well-known collec-
tions. She blames her current adventures in designing with two sharp pointy sticks entirely on a fellow
artist who, on seeing her knitting one day, asked her to design something for a gallery they were both a
part of... and one thing led to another, as they say.

In 2010, Hilary launched CRIMINAL KNITS, *a hugely popular and hilariously funny group on the knitting site Ravelry, to showcase her devious knitting designs in the form of Mystery knit-a-longs.*

Are you done yet? This is embarrassing.

Not quite.

Oh...

You can find CRIMINAL KNITS at http://www.ravelry.com/groups/criminal-knitsfor-the-serial-knitter-in-all -of-us.

You can find Hilary's other ebooks and individual knitting patterns in her Ravelry shop at http:// www.ravelry.com/designers/threebagsfulled.

Made in the USA
Columbia, SC
21 April 2019